The West Cumbria Flood Disaster 2009

A Photographic Account of Cockermouth and Workington

by Richard L. M. Byers

LANDMARKLIBRARIUM

FIRST PUBLISHED in December 2009 by
Landmark Librarium (an imprint of TYFH Publishing Limited)

TYFH Publishing Limited
Fletcher House, Moresby Parks
Whitehaven, Cumbria CA28 8XH

www.tyfh.net

ISBN 9780953844784
Landmark Guide # 04/002

British Library Cataloguing in Publication Data
A catalogue record of this book is available from the British Library.

ERRORS and OMISSIONS
Whilst the greatest care has been taken in the preparation of this book, th
publishers cannot be held responsible for any errors or omissions.

Front cover photograph shows rescue workers at the corner
of Sullart Street and Main Street, Cockermouth on the
morning of Friday 20th November 2009.

Introduction

ON THURSDAY 19 NOVEMBER 2009, England's worst recorded day of rain occurred across the fells of the Lake District. Over 314mm - more than one foot - fell at Seathwaite in the picturesque Borrowdale valley in just 24 hours, a level of rainfall described as a 1 in a 1000 year event. This prolonged and exceptionally heavy rain engulfed the becks and streams that tumble down the mountain slopes and swelled the lakes and rivers to unprecedented levels.

Ferocious floods rose at an alarming rate causing unimaginable devastation. Rivers burst their banks and surged through nearly 1400 homes in Keswick, Cockermouth and Workington, wreaking havoc for the stunned residents, leaving them homeless and totally heartbroken. Shops and businesses were engulfed and livelihoods ruined, at a time when their owners were already struggling to cope with the deepest recession since the 1930s.

Substantial bridges were washed away or damaged beyond repair, leaving the infra-structure of West Cumbria in total disarray. One of the greatest scenes of destruction was the collapse of Northside Bridge at Workington as the River Derwent reached exceptional levels. Here the heroic police officer, PC Bill Barker was swept to his death as the road bridge crumbled into the fast flowing waters.

For many days, West Cumbria became the centre of global media attention as the region struggled to come to terms with the tragic aftermath of this historic event. Now the cameras have left it is clear that there will be no quick fix solutions to massive problems the flooded families and businesses now face, it will be six to twelve months before they can realistically hope to return to their properties, some may never return. With no road bridges remaining over the River Derwent, between Papcastle and Workington, communities are split and face an 18 mile detour just to cross back and forth across the river, normally a distance of a few hundred yards. This road journey is also tortuous and slow as motorists frequently face long traffic jams in both directions.

The Cumbria Community Foundation set up a special Cumbria Flood Recovery Fund within 24 hours of the disaster. Thanks to the generosity of the general public, local businesses, the County Council and Allerdale Borough Council, the Cumbria Flood Recovery Fund has raised £1.2 million as the first edition of this book goes to print. I have also pledged all my royalties from the sale of this book to the fund.

We know from history that we have had similar storms but they already appear to becoming much more frequent and more destructive. Only time will tell whether the floods were a truly 'biblical', once in a lifetime event, or a sign that the predictions for Global Warming were correct and that we must brace ourselves for ever more frequent and devastating weather?

I sincerely hope that we in West Cumbria do not suffer the wrath of nature again on this scale for a very, very long time indeed.

Richard L. M. Byers
December 2009

A Photographic Account of Cockermouth and Workington

Photographers

Richard L M Byers
Andy V Byers
Becx Carter

After many days of wet weather, further unprecedented rainstorms fell across the Lake District on Thursday 19th November. This image captures a swollen River Greta at Keswick, having burst its banks and engulfed the adjacent Fitz Park. The Greta drains the southern slopes of fells such as Skiddaw and Blencathra, as well as the Threlkeld valley. ∎   photograph ©Becx Carter (info@rebecca-carter.com)

Another view of the River Greta, looking north west across Keswick's Fitz Park on the afternoon of 19th November. Here the water level rose rapidly and also engulfed several properties along Penrith Road. The footbridge over the River Greta is to the left of the photograph. ■   photograph ©Becx Carter (info@rebecca-carter.com)

In what is normally a busy part of Keswick's town centre, roads quickly became inpassable. Looking up Park Road, with Booths Supermarket to the right, the stranded delivery van presents a grim sight. Nearby premises in Crosthwaite Road also suffered major flood damage. ■   photograph ©Becx Carter (info@rebecca-carter.com)

Looking west along Cockermouth's Main Street, from Cocker Bridge, early on Friday 20th November. Although the water level has receded by around 600mm, the flood waters are still surging down the wide tree-lined street. ■

Flood waters pour into Main Street, Cockermouth, through the properties on either side of Cocker Bridge. Distressed residents watch in horror, but with the River Cocker still in full flood it will be many hours before the true extent of the damage can be safely seen. ■

Looking west towards Cockermouth's Cocker Bridge on the morning of Friday 20th November. The flood water continues to pour relentlessly into the town's Market Place. ∎

Top - A view across the flooded car park and the River Cocker, with the HSBC Bank in the distance. ■
Bottom - Looking down Ccokermouth's Market Place after the flood water had receeded and the clean up operation was about to begin. ■

The catastrophic flooding of the River Cocker as it winds its way through the Lorton valley to Cockermouth swept away almost everything in its path. Lorton bridge was completely washed away along with numerous trees. On Friday morning, as daylight broke and the waters receeded, a large tree was found lodged against the south side of Cocker Bridge. It had smashed its way through the cast iron railings and damaged the parapet wall of this Grade II listed bridge, build in 1828. ∎

An 80 ton crane on the east side of Cocker Bridge lifts the huge tree which was lodged against the bridge. In all nearly 8 tons of tree debris was removed from the river at this point. ∎

A torrent of water flows relentlessly through the open door of Percy House, in Market Place. Reputed to be Cockermouth's oldest town house, dating back to about 1390. The ground floor was extensively flooded. Thankfully, its priceless carved Elizabethan plaster ceiling to the upper floor was not damaged. ∎

Here at the foot of Castlegate the water was at its deepest in Cockermouth's Market Place. As water levels fell the full scale of the devastation became evident. Properties were flooded upto 1.5m deep and debris swept along by the torrent smashed through the shop windows and destroyed their contents. ■

A small brass plaque on the left hand side of the entrance into J. B. Banks Ironmongers in Market Place, records the level of a previous flood on the 13th August 1966 at 45cm. Flood waters at this point rose to 150cm on the 19th November 2009. ■

Further evidence of the damage to properties throughout Cockermouth. The flood waters have ripped through Portofino's Bistro, leaving a trail of destruction and dispair for its owner, Michael Stanley.■

Another image, looking towards the foot of Castlegate, from Cocker Bridge. Portofino's Bistro is on the right of the photograph, next to Colin Graham's 'Curiosity Shop'. Within this antique shop the water rose about 600mm above street level. ■

In the aftermath of the exceptional flooding and devastation, Cockermouth and Workington became the centre of attention from the world's media. 24 hour news channels broadcasted countless live news reports from the two towns. All the rooms in several local hotels were also fully booked by the television companies for almost a week.■

Looking from Lowther Went down the lane into a flooded Main Street at 10.00 am on Friday morning. The flood waters swept up the many narrow lanes on either side of the street inundating properties. ∎

Cockermouth's Main Street was exposed to the full force of the flooding. By 9.00pm on Thursday evening it was a torrent. During the night the Fire Service and RAF helicopters evacuated around 200 residents to safety, as the water rose at an alarming rate. ■

Beer barrels and other debris float along Main Street at its junction with Sullart Street, as one of the many inflatable rescue boats sets off on a further mission to search for any forgotten flood victims. ■

The Georgian interior of Wordsworth House, the childhood home of William and Dorothy Wordsworth, escaped major flood damage. In this photograph we can see the water level very close to the top of the steps. But the Cafe in the adjacent old stable block and the National Trust shop were submerged under several feet of water. ■

A view of the rear of Wordsworth House where the flood water did engulf the period garden and caused major damage to the terraced walk overlooking the River Derwent. The long high stone wall along the river side of the terrace collapsed when the fast flowing waters undermined its foundations. ■

Another view of the flood damage to the terraced walk at the rear of Cockermouth's Wordsworth House. Here William Wordsworth once played as a young boy, with his sister Dorothy. The poet later wrote "....the bright blue river passed along the margin of our terraced walk; A tempting playmate whom we dearly loved."

Top - A view down Low Sands Lane towards the rear of Wordsworth House after the flood waters had receeded.
Bottom - The rescue operations were co-ordinated from the fire station head-quarters. Emergency vehicles lined the streets around the war memorial, seen to the right of this picture. ∎

A view down Station Street towards its flooded junction with Main Street. By Thursday at 4.00pm the water was waist high in Main Street, but it later rose to over 2 metres at this point. ■

A worried and concerned Tony Cunningham, the MP for Workington, was in Cockermouth on Thursday evening at the height of the floods and again on Friday to survey the devastation. He would later greet many high profile visitors to the region, including Prince Charles, Prime Minister Gordon Brown, Enviroment Secretary Hilary Benn, Local Government Minister Rosie Winterton, Transport Minister Sidiq Khan and Sarah Brown, plus numerous other Government civil servants and representatives. ■

Looking downstream from Cocker Bridge, with the old Courthouse to the left of the photograph. The swollen River Cocker has risen dramatically to engulf the 'Honest Lawyer' Bistro and Wine Bar, which is well below the bridge level. In the distance is the rear of Jennings Brewery where flood water rose to well over a metre. Brewing production is unlikely to re-commence until January 2010. ∎

The north section of the Mill footbridge (erected in 1981) collapsed into the River Derwent at Cockermouth, when the flood waters swept away the supporting stonework pillar. To the left is the Derwent Mills, water rose to ankle deep on the ground floor by 3.45pm on Thursday, when the residents were evacuated. ■

The Riverside Car Park at Cockermouth was flooded with several feet of water as the River Cocker burst its banks. ■

Two contrasting views of the arched entrance to the Riverside Car Park, taken just a few days apart. The top photograph shows the flood waters on Friday morning. Eyewitnesses revealed that on Thursday night, the height of the water had almost reached the top of the smaller arches. ∎

Looking west from the churchyard of All Saints Church, high above the swollen River Cocker. In the foreground is the flooded Riverside Car Park. ■

View of the Croftside properties from the foot of Cocker Lane, taken on Friday morning. Note the flood debris that has been deposited against the footbridge to the left of the photograph. ∎

A photograph looking along the Croftside bank of the River Cocker, taken just two days after the floods receeded. Here flood waters rose to almost the balcony level of the first floor. ∎

A view looking down Cocker Lane, across the River Cocker, at first light on Friday morning. The swollen river has burst its banks and submerged numerous properties in Challoner Street and Croftside, on the opposite side of the bridge. The structure of the footbridge is choked with debris as the turbulent waters flow relentlessly past. ■

A photograph of the footbridge crossing the River Cocker at the bottom of Cocker Lane, taken during the summer of 2007. This bridge can be seen on the previous page almost totally submerged in the fast flowing flood waters. ■

Another view across the turbulent and swollen River Cocker, looking towards the flood stricken properties on Rubbybanks Road, taken on Friday morning. ■

The foaming, brown muddy flood waters still roar under the Victoria Jubilee Bridge on Friday morning. Just hours earlier they were at least a metre higher at this point. ■

Looking north from Cockermouth's Victoria Jubilee Bridge the river has risen above the flood defences and engulfed the properties along Rubbybanks Road, to the left of the photograph. ■

Steve Lambert stands ankle deep in the water outside his house on Rubbybanks Road, early on Friday morning. Inside his flood-damaged home is a scene of utter devastation. At its height the water rose almost a metre above the internal floor level. ■

The location of each of the bridges along the River Derwent at Workington is identified on this map. The Dock Railway Bridge is shown as (A), The Main Line Railway Bridge (B), Northside Bridge (C), Navvies Bridge (D), Workington Bridge (E) and the site of the new temporary footbridge (F). ■

A view of the north section of Dock Quay, after the waters had receeded. Here debris in the fast flowing river caused major damage to several of its reinforced concrete bridge supports, causing the structure to bend and buckle. The railway bridge and the public footpath which runs along its seaward side were closed for safety reasons. ∎

A similar 2007 photograph of the Dock Bridge, in the foreground is the sandstone wall which extended from the end of Merchants Quay to the centre of the bridge. This was almost completely washed away by the ferocious floods. We can see what now remains of Merchants Quay to the right of the top photograph. ∎

As the destructive floods washed away or damaged all the bridges across the River Derwent at Workington, with the exception of just the railway bridge. Network Rail reacted quickly and built a temporary station near Dunmail Park. The new station called 'Workington North', opened on Monday 30th November. ■

The extra rail services between Workington and Maryport, stopping at the new Workington North Station are operated by DRS and hauled by Class 47 diesel locomotives. The rolling stock includes luxury first class carriages, which are normally used to take passengers to Royal Ascot. ■

A view of the railway bridge over the River Derwent at Workington, at first light on Friday 20th November. Engineers inspect the structure as the powerful floodwaters sweep by just a few feet below. Railway journeys suffered minor disruption compared to other forms of travel. ■   photograph © Andy V. Byers

Another image of Workington's railway bridge clearly showing its construction. Supported on fourteen cylindrical iron columns the girder bridge survived any major damage. Built in 1845, the bridge was once part of the Whitehaven Junction Railway. ■

Northside Bridge, viewed from the Derwent End of Borough Park, just a few hours after its collapse. Workington's lifeboat was launched to search for PC Bill Barker. But it was not until much later on Friday that his body was discovered on the beach, near Crosscanonby.■   photograph © Andy V. Byers

Taken after the flood waters receeded this photograph reveals the devastation of the Northside Bridge. The 12.2m wide sandstone bridge was built between 1901-3.■

An aerial photograph of Northside Bridge that collapsed on Friday 20th November at the height of the flooding. This was the scene of the greatest devastation and claimed the life of PC Bill Barker, who was swept away as the substantial bridge crumbled into the swollen waters of the River Derwent. ■

PC Bill Barker (1964-2009), who tragically lost his life in the floods while helping others, just a day before his 45th birthday. He was later described by the Prime Minister, Gordon Brown as 'very brave, very heroic'. ■

Looking north over the site of Northside Bridge. When the bridge collapsed and Workington Bridge was closed as unsafe, traffic had a 18 mile detour via Papcastle Bridge (Cockermouth) just to cross back and forth across the River Derwent, normally a distance of a few hundred yards. ∎

Flood waters on the Cloffolks rose to within inches of the council offices at Allerdale House. Yet the remainder of the Cloffolks, including the proposed site of a new 'Tesco Extra' store was flooded by upto 600mm. One wonders if the supermarket will still be built or the plans revised. ∎

photograph © Andy V. Byers.

The south section of Navvies footbridge collapsed into the River Derwent in the early hours of friday morning, as its massive supporting sandstone pillar was simply washed away by the extraordinary power of the swollen river. Navvies bridge was a former railway bridge built in 1878. ■

This view of the surviving section of Navvies bridge on the northside of the River Derwent shows the remaining pillar, identical in size to the one on the other side of the river that was washed away. ■

Workington Police Station was also submerged when the River Derwent burst its banks, rendering it unusable during the emergency operations. Quick thinking staff moved virtually everything to safety. The building was only closed until the 2nd December, with officers working from Whitehaven Station and the Territorial Army Centre on Harrington Road.■ photograph © Andy V. Byers

Looking west across a flooded Curwen Park through the trees to the foot of Hall Brow. Here the water level rose well above the wall surrounding the park. The nearby Cricket Club and Bowling Club were also standing under 600mm (2ft) of water by first light on Friday morning.■ photograph © Andy V. Byers

Looking north from the foot of Hall Brow in Workington, towards Hall Park View. This part of the town has always been suspect to flooding, but here the waters rose rapidly to levels never before seen in living memory. The River Derwent burst its banks around 6.00pm on the Thursday evening. ■

A view of Hall Park View in the aftermath of the flooding. Rows of skips piled high with the residents' sodden and contaminated furniture and belongings line the street. ■

The mill race which winds its way from the Hall Mill to the South Gut at Workington harbour, passes behind the homes at Hall Park View. At the height of the floods it was engulfed by the fast flowing waters of the River Derwent causing substantial destruction. ∎

Another later view of Hall Park View in Workington. The Army lorries are part of a convoy carrying thousands of tons of hardcore to the site of the new temporary footbridge. Obscured by the lorries, a large section of the wall around Curwen Park has been washed away by the flood waters. ∎

The floods wreaked further havoc severely damaging Workington Bridge at the foot of Calva Brow. The bridge was closed to all traffic. For days, Workington was the focus of the world's media as it was feared the collapse of the 168 year old, Grade II listed structure was imminent. ∎

As the water level in the River Derwent receeds the true extent of the damage to Workington Bridge is revealed. This view of the east side shows a major crack (A) and large sections of stonework at the base of the southern support have been dislodged or washed away (B). ∎   photograph © Andy V. Byers

Residents of the small community of Barepot on the north side of the River Derwent were evacuated from their homes at around 7pm on Thursday evening as the river broke its banks and the flood water rose at an alarming rate. ■

Royal Engineer Godfrey Manduwi in Workington's Mill Field, sets out the site of the new temporary footbridge across the River Derwent. The 4.2m wide bridge, constructed from Mabey & Johnston panels, is intended for pedestrian and cyclists only, but could also carry emergency vehicles.■   photograph © Andy V. Byers

Troops unload the bulky rolls of TriAx geogrid, used to stabilise the soft marshy ground of Mill Field, beneath the hardcore of the new car park and turning area. Here the 51.85m long bridge was constructed from pre-fabricated sections. The Army had previously build several almost identical structures in the Helmand provinces of war-torn Afghanistan. ■ photograph ©Andy V Byers

The soldiers of the local TA, Royal Engineers, Royal Logistic Corps, Royal Signals and Royal Military Police assembled the new temporary footbridge, located about 300m east of the condemned Workington Bridge. ■ photograph ©Andy V Byers

A view looking due west beneath the new temporary footbridge as it is pushed on rollers across the River Derwent. In the distance is the crippled pillar of Workington Bridge, built in 1841. Between these two structures was the site of an earlier bridge built in 1763. ■

photograph ©Andy V Byers

The completed temporary footbridge installed in just over a week by the Army, reunites the isolated communities of Northside, Seaton and Barepot on the north bank of the River Derwent with the remainder of the town. Officially opened just after 8.05am on Monday 7th December, the bridge was named 'Barker Crossing', in memory of PC Bill Barker who tragically lost his life at the height of the floods, just seventeen days earlier. ■

How it all happened

MUCH OF THE BEAUTY of Cumbria is generally provided by the pictur-esque lakes, the rivers that flow through the valleys and the little becks that meander down the bracken covered slopes of the fells. The majority of visitors see them in summer when the lakes are inevitably low and the streams are a tiny trickle.

These streams in their dozens drain the high moorland and feed the largest rivers, which in turn empty into the lakes. The three major rivers that flow through West Cumbria are the Derwent, Cocker and the Greta. The River Derwent has its source above Sprinkling Tarn, in the shadow of Great Gable, high above the Borrowdale valley. It winds its way north for about six miles, through Seathwaite, Seatoller and Grange, before first draining into Derwent Water. At the north of the lake near Keswick, it reappears for about three miles, before feeding into Bassenthwaite Lake. At Ouse Bridge the River Derwent begins the final stage of its journey winding back and forth through Cockermouth and west to the Solway estuary at Workington.

The River Greta has its origins in the Threlkeld valley below the steep slopes of Blencathra as a modest series of streams. As it falls west towards Keswick, several other becks drain into the Greta, from the surrounding fells and St John's in the Vale. The River Cocker begins at the north end of Crummock Water, which is fed by Loweswater and Buttermere. Buttermere has its origins in the high fells to the west of Honister Pass. The Cocker flows through the Lorton Valley to meet the River Derwent, in the centre of Cockermouth, close to the castle.

Before the devastating floods, rainfall in the Lake District during November 2009 was already unusually high and the ground was very wet and sodden. Even a short dry spell, or perhaps the cessation of rain for a day or so gave little respite. The weather forecast for Thursday 19th November was again for prolonged and very heavy rain across the north west of England, but with periods of widespread torrential rain over the Cumbrian Fells. It is calculated that the intensity was about 100mm (or 4inches) in one single hour, and subsequently over 314mm (over 1 foot) was measured at Seathwaite in the twenty-four hours. One foot! More than three months' normal rainfall.

But this catastrophe of nature was not isolated to a small area, it occurred across the Lake District. As well as in West Cumbria, 1.5m (5ft) floods occurred at Waterhead, Ambleside and water rose to an amazing 4.2m (12ft) at Coniston. Becks that in summer were a mere trickle became broad streams, streams soon became larger. At first, the streams overflowed their normal channels and spread out on either side of the banks, sweeping over the meadowland and low-lying countryside. As it continued to rain, this ever increasing and phenomenal volume of water flowed into the major rivers, and they combined their power to become ferocious fast-flowing torrents. The natural result is rivers will rise, and they rise quickly. First, saplings and the rough growth at the rivers' edge were torn away. The angry waters then tore at bigger obstacles. Large trees, boulders and anything that impeded the progress of the flood were carried away. The very weight of this material, as well as the immense power of the water, swept aside other obstructions.

The River Greta at Keswick was the first to burst its banks, flooding Fitz Park and the properties around Penrith Road. Closer to the town centre, as the line of the Greta turns through two 90 degree bends, behind the former Cumberland Pencil factory, the waters engulfed High Hill. The River Cocker also gained in intensity as the rainstorm continued to fall across the Buttermere Fells. Lorton Bridge was washed away, as the river waters rose rapidly and raced towards Cockermouth.

So the roaring Cocker converged with the equally swollen and angry River Derwent at Cockermouth. Widespread flooding was clearly inevitable as the waters rose quickly and wreaked further havoc in its path. Main Street and Market Place were exposed to the full force of the flood as the fast flowing waters surged through hundreds of properties. Rescue teams worked throughout the night and several RAF helicopters made countless flights, airlifting the devastated inhabitants to safety.

The River Derwent then heads towards Workington, following almost the same line as the A66. Despite overflowing vast areas of low-lying ground either side of its path, the Derwent also met the rising evening tide at its estuary. As a result the already swollen and violent flood waters continued to rise further sweeping through the small community of Barepot and across Mill Field, Curwen Park and the Cloffolks. Many bridges were swept away or critically damaged, but the greatest scene of devastation was when Northside Bridge collapsed.

ACKNOWLEDGMENTS

The author wishes to acknowledge with grateful thanks, the kind assistance and contributions offered by Jo E. Byers, Andy V. Byers, Becx Carter and Michael Burridge. Finally, a very special thank you to everyone I spoke to, who had experienced the catastrophic floods of the 19th - 20th November 2009. Your input proved invaluable and essential in order to do this book justice.
Best wishes to all for the future.

Prince Charles Message to Cumbria

ON A TWO-DAY TRIP to flood affected Cumbria, Prince Charles visited Workington, Keswick and Cockermouth. At Workington he called into the Northside Community Centre before heading to Keswick to meet the flood victims and those involved in the rescue operation. Later that evening, in front of a cheering crowd he helped switch on the Christmas lights at Keswick, with television celebrity Julia Bradbury.

The following day he toured the flood devastation in Cockermouth and again met the rescue teams. In a private meeting he also met the wife and children of the late PC Bill Barker.

In a special message to the people of Cumbria he wrote:

"I HAVE NOTHING but the greatest possible sympathy for all those affected by the latest appalling floods. I can well imagine the devastation these will have caused, but as a regular visitor to Cumbria I have personal experience of the strength of the community spirit which exists in this most beautiful of counties.

It has been incredibly heartening to see how everyone – from the emergency services and volunteer groups to friends and neighbours – have worked together to provide the kind of mutual support necessary to get through this most terrible of ordeals.

I am only too aware that recovery will take time, particularly for those rural communities which have found themselves isolated from the services of nearby towns.

I do so hope that local businesses and the agricultural community might find a way to work together not only to ensure their revival, but also to help those most in need.

For this reason, I have asked one or two of Britain's most senior business leaders to come with me on my visit today so they can see at first hand what the particular problems and challenges are in case they might be able to do anything to help.

I realise that, unfortunately, it will take many months before all the damage from last week's floods is repaired. This work will obviously challenge everyone, but I have no doubt you will face this test with resilience and fortitude. My thoughts and prayers are with you all."

HRH Prince Charles
November 2009

Cumbria Flood Recovery Appeal

THE FOUNDATION WAS able to start making emergency grants from the fund to help flood victims just four days after the floods hit. So far, they have given out 123 grants totalling £75,450 with many more applications in the pipeline and hundreds more anticipated in the months ahead as people slowly recover from the crisis. Grant aid is also available for groups organising activities and other support services for flood victims.

A flood victim who had just been given a grant from the Cumbria Flood Recovery Fund, recently sent the following email. We were so touched by its contents that we wanted to pass it on to you in its entirety. It says so much about how important community is at times of crisis. It is also a big thank you to all those who have donated to the Cumbria Flood Recovery Fund so far.

"I have just received a cheque to help cover some of my losses in the flood, and I want to offer my sincerest thanks for the kind gesture, for which I am hugely appreciative. I have been very much alone throughout this experience, due to my family being so far away, and have had to rely upon the generosity of some friends I have in the area, and whatever else help I could get. I was so impressed with the help that I received from community organisations such as yourselves, who gave me fantastic advice during what has been a very difficult and traumatic time for myself. I am so thankful to those friendly faces, who took the time to listen. It gives me great confidence to know that the community in which I live and work can provide such stability and support to those who need it, and when they need it most. I am overwhelmed with gratitude to those individuals who gave their time to help, and hugely thankful for the efforts of the Cumbria Community Foundation and the excellent work it does. If possible, please pass on my thanks to all those concerned.
Kindest regards
M. Cockermouth"

To apply for grant aid from the Fund or to make a donation please visit www.cumbriafoundation.org or telephone 01900 825760 for assistance.

THE AUTHOR

Richard Byers is an experienced local historian and author with many books to his credit, these include:

History of Workington - Earliest Times to 1865 (ISBN 095298122X)
History of Workington - 1866 to 1955 (ISBN 0952981254)
Workington from the Air - Past & Present (ISBN 0952981246)
Workington War Heroes (ISBN 0953844765)
Workington Iron & Steel (ISBN 075243196X)
Images of England - Workington (ISBN 0752432958)
Workington Then & Now (ISBN 0752437445)
Moss Bay, Workington - The End of the Line

He has also edited the following titles:

Bradbury's History of Cockermouth (ISBN 0952981203)
Sugden's History of Arlecdon & Frizington (ISBN 0952981211)
Bessemer Steel - Steelmaking at Workington (ISBN 0953844714)
Dickinson's Dictionary of Cumberland Dialect (ISBN 0953844773)

www.richardbyers.co.uk